I HATE YOU
YOU

ALL

Eldar Stein

Introduction

Do you know that feeling when you wake up in the morning and you're already in a funk before the day has even started?

Or the feeling that you want to emigrate right now because there are only idiots working around you?

Do you ever wonder why fate has to test your patience so often?
If you answered yes to any of these questions, this book is for you, because you can't get rid of all the stupid or annoying people in your life.

But you can get rid of your frustration and pent-up aggression by completing the pages in this book, and the tasks, some of which are funny, snappy, or relaxing, will immediately lower your stress level.

You will become calmer and more relaxed, and you will be able to look at your situation with a sense of humor. With that in mind, I wish you a lot of fun filling out this book.

And always remember: everything will work out fine in the end. If it's not good, it's not the end.

OHHHHHM !

Draw pins in all the places where you want the person the voodoo doll represents to feel pain, and write a name above the doll if you like.

Write down who or what annoyed you the most today.

1) _____

2) _____

3) _____

4) _____

5) _____

5

Whose sleeves should fall down while washing dishes?

_____

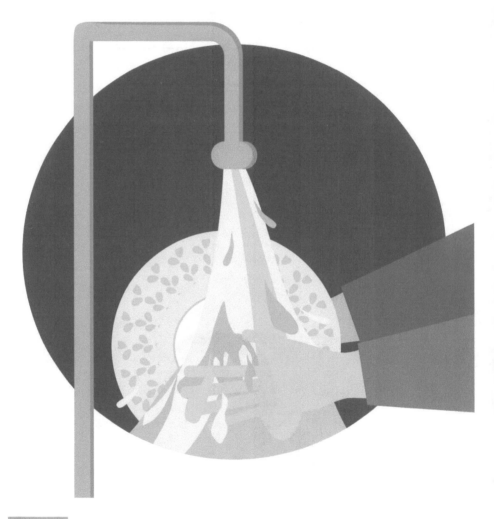

6

Color this middle finger and imagine
who you would like to show it to.

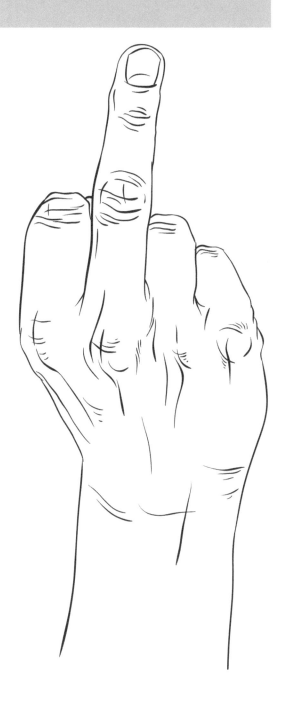

Who should have an itchy nose when he/she has his/her hands full?

_____

Solve this maze and take a deep breath. There is only one way.

This bus is going to hell. Add a nice pur-
gatory and draw people who should go
with it.

Draw these doodles with a
sharp pencil

WORDSHIP: Find as many swear words as you can!

A P I D I O T Z R E

J V T R V Q R W P P

A S S H O L E C B M

C Y S R H O T K A A

K W M N V O T Z S L

A Q P I S S E R T H

S W P S S E L L A C

S X M L F R G J R S

E K E U G H B P D Y

T X K T F U C K P R

Draw your version of a stupid pig here!

Draw your version of a stupid cow here.

This is Fuck the Bat. Con-
nect the dots with a pencil
and bring Fuck to life.

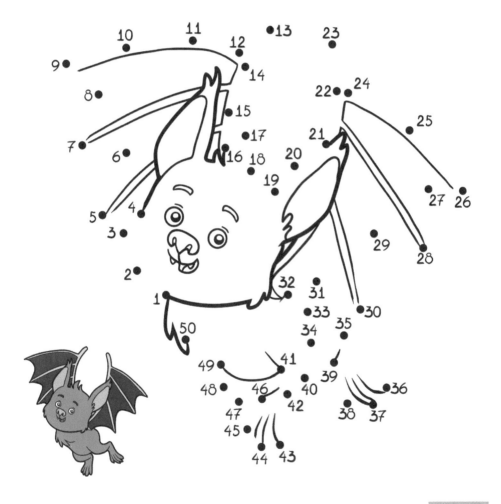

Check which of the options you find more corrosive.

☐ Cold coffee	☐ Warm beer
☐ Itchy nose	☐ Pimples on chin
☐ moldy bread	☐ annoying colleagues
☐ Overtime	☐ Boredom
☐ Christmas party	☐ Company party
☐ stupid people	☐ lazy people
☐ Lurker	☐ Speeders
☐ Birdshot	☐ Poop on shoe
☐ Meeting	☐ Presentation

There are no stupid questions? Oh, yes, there are. Write down the stupidest questions you've ever been asked.

Stupid sayings: Write down all the stupid sayings that drive you up the wall on a regular basis.

Doodle free! Draw wild zig-zag lines here until the page is full.

Draw yourself free. Draw wild serpentine lines until the page is full.

Color this mandala while yelling.

DARTBOARD: Put the book down and throw a sharp pencil at this dartboard. Repeat as many times as you like.

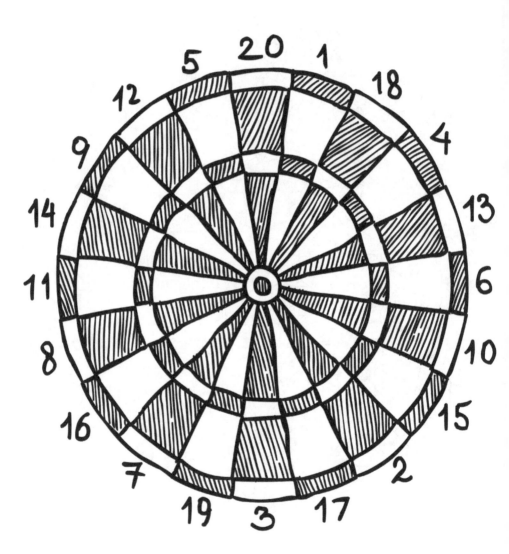

This is GRUMPY. Cut out Grumpy and hang him somewhere as a motivational animal.

WINNER'S DRIVE: Draw or write down who tops the list of most annoying people in your life.

Bread can mold and what can you?
Write here the names of people who have even less on them than this bread.

You are as good as Photoshop.
Make this woman beautiful (paint
pimples, glasses, beard, etc.)

You are as good as Photoshop.
Make this man beautiful (paint
pimples, glasses, beard, etc.)

How much patience do you have left for today? Cut out the hourglass that most closely matches your level of patience.

This is the red card for annoying people. Cut out the picture and give it to
someone who is annoying you. That
person has to shut up for five minutes.

Who is dumber than the police allow and should be in jail for it?

_____

Cut out this sign and post it in a promi-
nent place (on your computer, for exam-
ple) so that everyone knows right away
that you don't want to be approached.

Do not talk
to Driver!

This is the „don't give a shit unicorn".
Write in the thought bubble what
you could give a shit about today.

This yoga pose is called „annoy-ed monkey". Sit cross-legged on the floor, extend your middle fingers and take three deep breaths in and out.

CONFETTI: Color the confetti temp-
lates, then cut them out with nail scis-
sors. When you're done, you'll be
calmer than you are now. I promise!

PAINTING: Paint this be-
autiful pile of shit and relax.

HEART BEAT: Draw your heart-
beat on this line when you think of
the most annoying person you know.

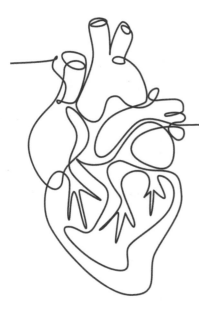

Cool down with a guessing game: Distract yourself when you need to get upset.

Which penguin
is reflecting
in the water?

Gratitude DAYBOOK: Write a few sentences here about what you are thankful for today.

I am grateful today that........

............I'm not such an idiot as ....

....

....

....

....

....

....

....

....

....

....

....

1. My job is like a circus and I am the **director**.

2. It's okay if you don't like me. Not **everyone** has good taste.

3. I type messages to annoying people **with** my middle finger.

4. Stupidity is also a natural talent.

5. If you get up earlier, you hate more of your day.

6. I am awake. The daily madness can **begin**.

7. I smile! I can't kill them all.

8. Stupidity begins where sarcasm is **no longer** understood.

....

....

....

....

....

....

This is the tombstone of a person who has annoyed you a lot in your life. Write the sentence on the tombstone that you think is most appropriate.

Draw more lines here on this
page until the page is full.

Who has a few fries short of a happy meal?

_____

Draw more circles here on
this page until the page is full.

Who would you like to shoot to the moon with this rocket?

_____

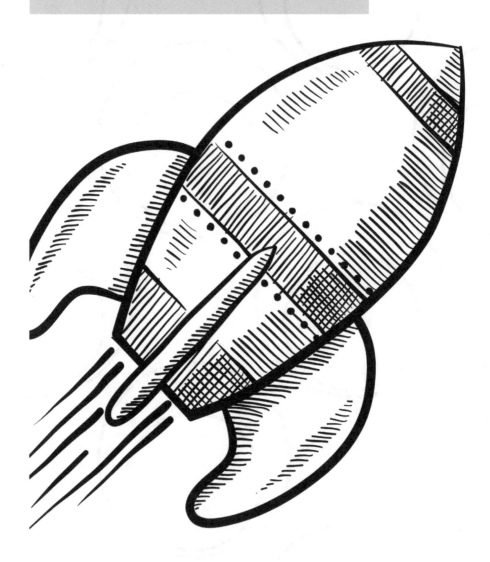

Draw more strokes here on this page
until the page is full.

Who bugs you?

_____

Draw more squares here on this page
until the page is full.

Circle the type of people you find most annoying.

neighbors

In-laws

Colleagues

Blabbermouth

Boss

Brother / sister in law

Bad drivers

Know-it-alls

Arrogant snobs

Ass kisser

Clients

48

List your top 5 most annoying songs here

1) _____

2) _____

3) _____

4) _____

5) _____

Who gets your goat?

_____

Dictionary: What you really mean when you talk to idiots.

What I say	What I mean
Good Morning.....	
I'm happy to do that for you......	
See you soon..........	
Kind regards........	
Dear Mr......... Dear Mrs............	
This sounds good.......	

Who has a screw loose?

_____

If you are feeling particularly angry or up-set, throw this book on the floor/against the wall or at annoying people.

Who is off your nuts?

_____

Take a pointed object and scratch a wild
pattern on this black surface.

Draw in the bug that you get, when someone bugs you. (it can be really big)

Color in these bacteria and viruses as you relax.

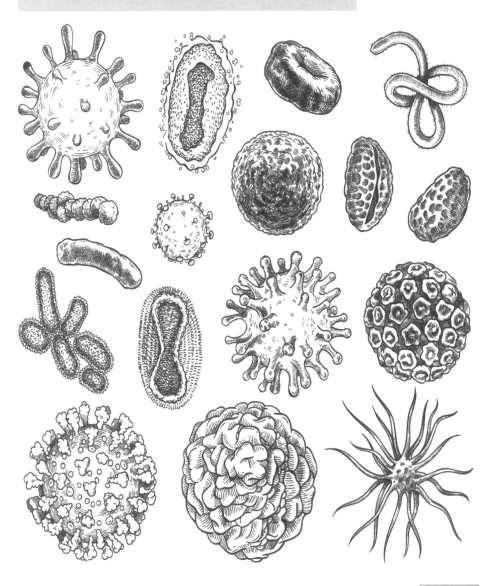

Every Whatsapp status is a silent message to someone. Write your status here for a particularly annoying person.

Scribble a different pattern in each circle as you calm down.

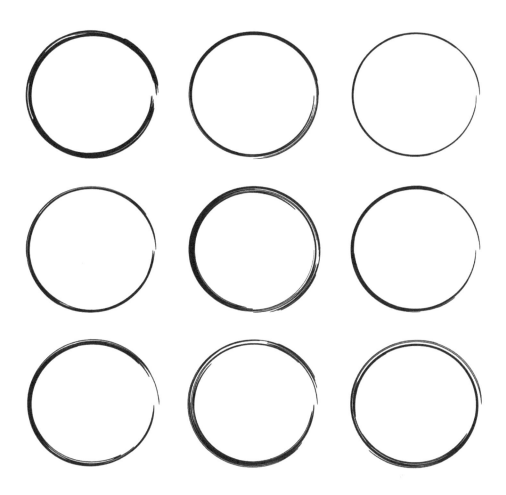

Ever wanted to learn how to draw a camel? Now you have the chance to prove it on the next page.

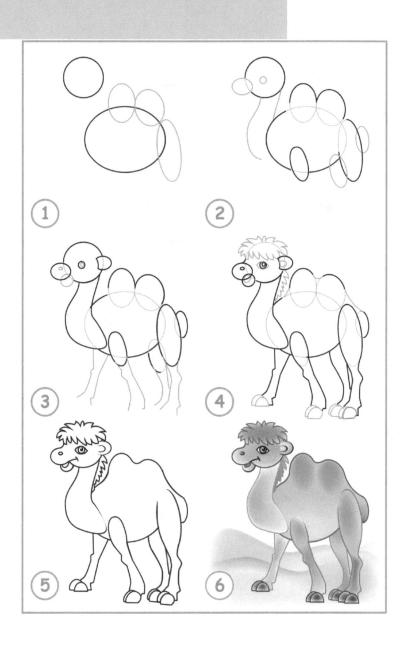

Paper Airplane: Use these instructions
to make a paper airplane. Tear out
the next page and fold it accordingly.

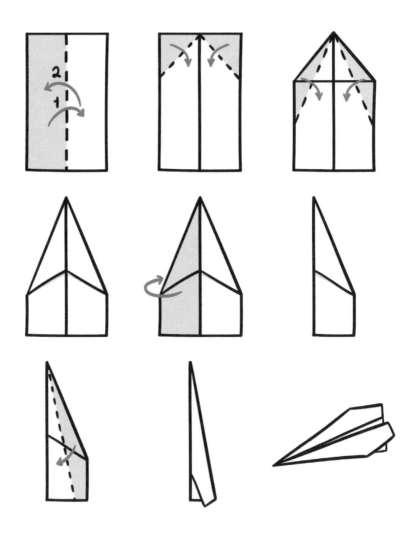

63

64

Scribble a different pattern in each square as you calm down.

Who is your pain in the neck?

_____

SUDOKU

Puzzle fun: Relieve tension and stress by solving this Sudoku puzzle. You can find the solution on the following page.

5	4			2		8		6
	1	9			7			3
			3			2	1	
9			4		5		2	
		1				6		4
6		4		3	2		8	
	6					1	9	
4		2		9				5
	9			7		4		2

Solution:

5	4	3	9	2	1	8	7	6
2	1	9	6	8	7	5	4	3
8	7	6	3	5	4	2	1	9
9	8	7	4	6	5	3	2	1
3	2	1	7	9	8	6	5	4
6	5	4	1	3	2	9	8	7
7	6	5	2	4	3	1	9	8
4	3	2	8	1	9	7	6	5
1	9	8	5	7	6	4	3	2

Draw this beautiful single-celled orga-
nism. Imagine a person as intelligent as
this creature.

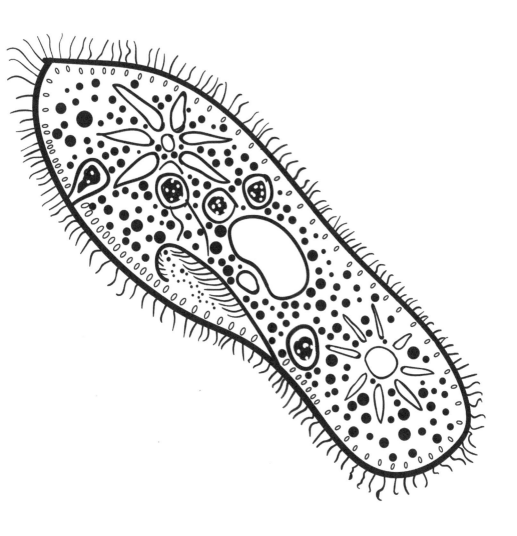

Who is as daft as a brush?

_____

Color this loon and think of a person who
is crazy as a loon.

ORIGAMI: Relax while you fold this pig.
Tear out the next page and use it for this.

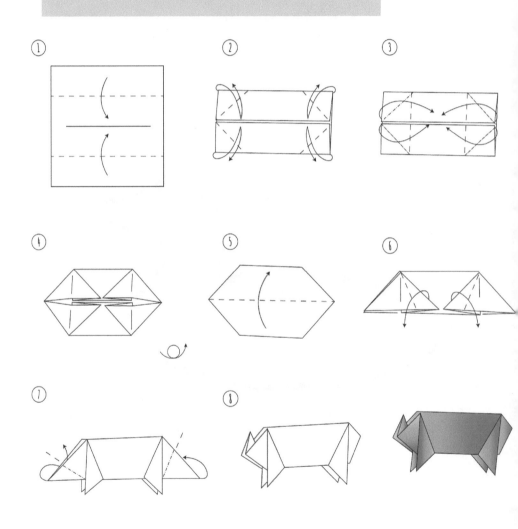

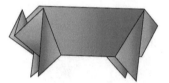

74

Color in these patterns while you relax.

Keep a tally sheet. Add a tally mark every time you get really excited.

Draw and/or cut out these symbols for your daily heroism.
Praise yourself today.

Who is as thick as two short planks?

_____

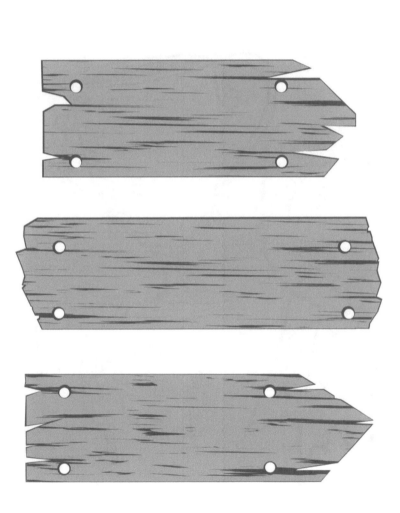

Relax and color this beautiful sloth.

Ohhhhm: cut out and relax.use nail scis-
sors to cut out these wonderful orna-
ments. By the time you're done, you'll
have forgotten what you were so excited
about :)

Color in this angry unicorn.

Who is a pain in the butt?

_____

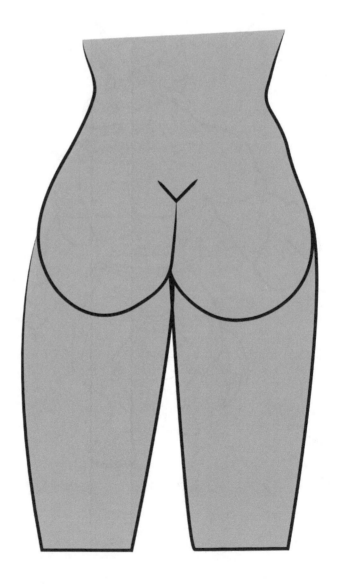

Create this beautiful tetrahedron by cutting and gluing this template.

etrahedral dice

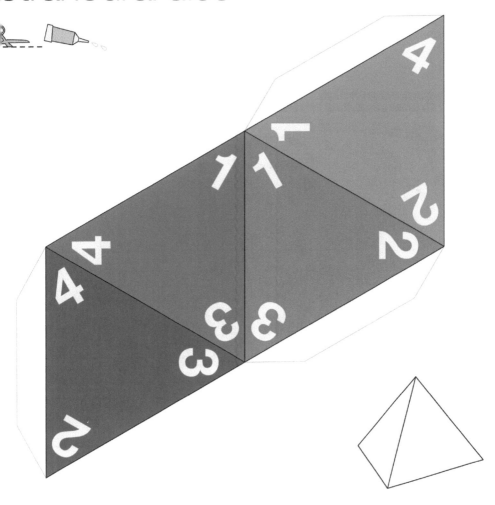

If your life were a series, what would it be called?

_____

Be creative and finish this drawing.

Who did not hear the shot?

_____

Color the letters in the appropriate colors.

BLUE

PINK

GREEN

RED

Draw an angry face on this unicorn.

Find 9 differences between the two pictu-
res. You will find the solution on the next
page.

Find 9 Differences!

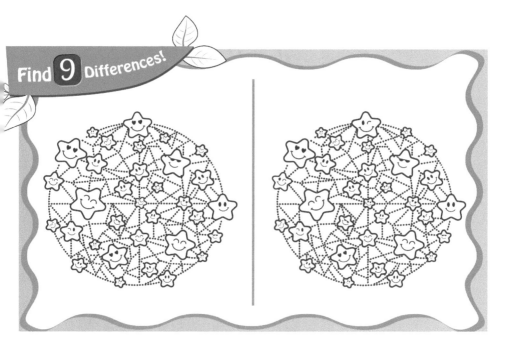

Solution:

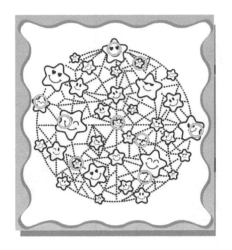

Feeling-O-Meter: Draw how you feel today.

PAIN MEASUREMENT SCALE

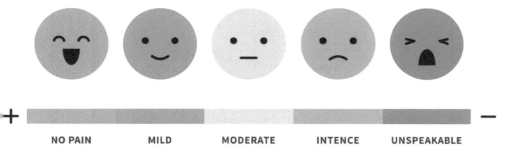

NO PAIN   MILD   MODERATE   INTENCE   UNSPEAKABLE

Surely you know some people who talk a
lot but have nothing to show for it.
Make this duck with tho-
se people in mind. QUACK!

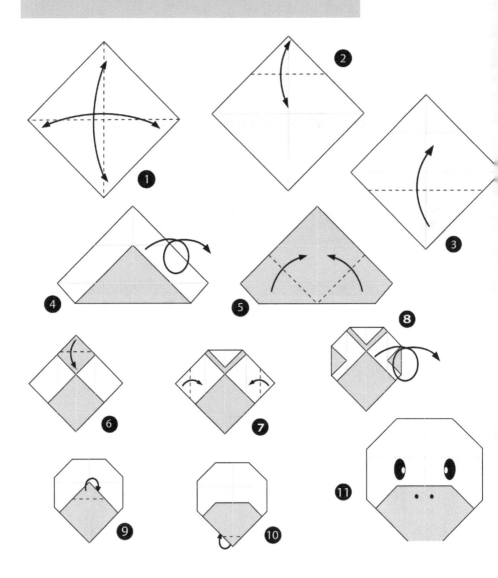

92

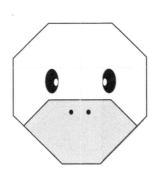

93

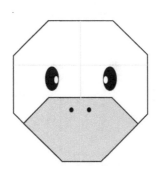

94

Did you know that jellyfish have no brains?
Surely you can think of some of your contemporaries whom you suspect of being jellyfish. As you think of these people, draw these jellyfish.

Who deserves a high five in the face?

_____

Draw here the inner thunderstorm wit-
hin you when you get upset again.

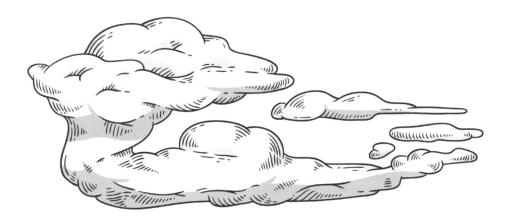

Here you can draw the animal that you will become when you get aroused.

Write here the thoughts that are on your
mind today.

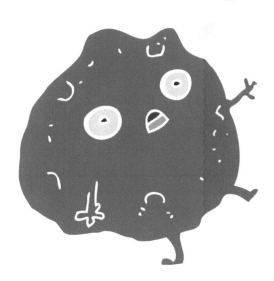

Poke holes in this page with a pencil.

Draw your hand here with a pencil
while showing your middle finger with

Paint a creative graffiti on the wall.

Draw your view out of the window here.

Who do you wish had chapped hands when they were squeezing the lemons?

_____

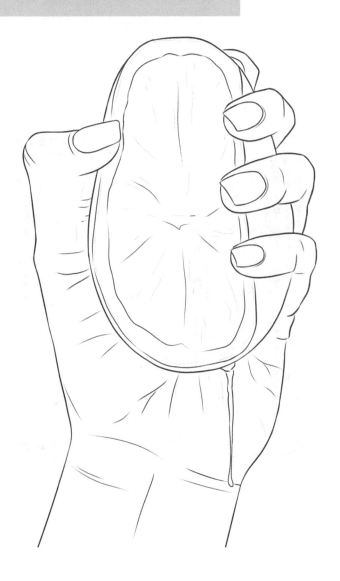

Who would you like to have cold coffee and warm beer forever?

_____

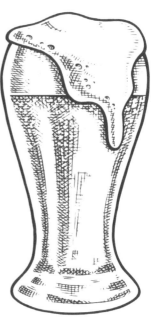

Who do you always want to have pinched underwear for?

_____

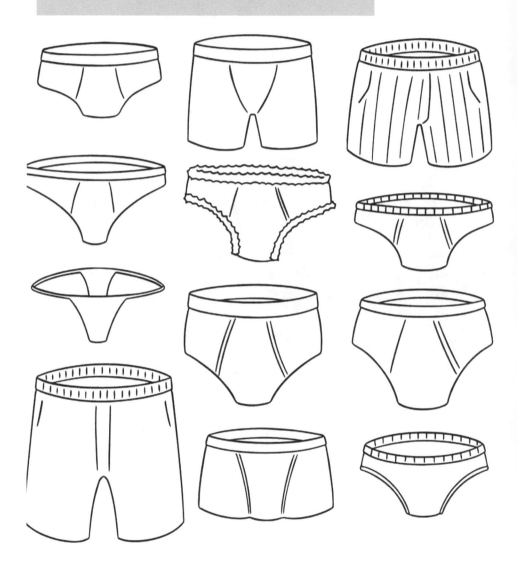

Color this beautiful curse picture while you relax.

Who do you wish had an empty roll of
toilet paper when you poop?

_____

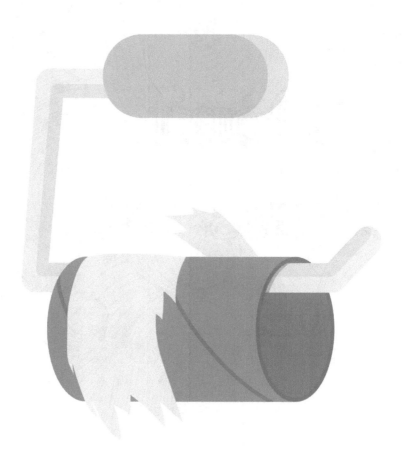

Solve this maze. There is only
one right way. You will find
the solution on the next page.

Solution:

On this and the following pages you can give free rein to your creativity and write, paint, doodle, whatever you like.

On this and the following pages you can give free rein to your creativity and write, paint, doodle, whatever you like.

On this and the following pages you
can give free rein to your creativity and
write, paint, doodle, whatever you like.

On this and the following pages you can give free rein to your creativity and write, paint, doodle, whatever you like.

On this and the following pages you can give free rein to your creativity and write, paint, doodle, whatever you like.

On this and the following pages you can give free rein to your creativity and write, paint, doodle, whatever you like.

On this and the following pages you can give free rein to your creativity and write, paint, doodle, whatever you like.

On this and the following pages you can give free rein to your creativity and write, paint, doodle, whatever you like.

On this page you can give free rein to your creativity and write, paint, doodle, whatever you like.

Made in United States
Troutdale, OR
11/15/2023